Dedicated to my Father God first! Without Whom this absolutely would not have been possible. Thank You Father for all Your BUT GODs in my life and Your Provision!

Also, my amazingly awesome support team: Paulette, Shwetha, Lei, Jess, Nadine, Mina, Shrunga, Diane, Rosie, and Audrey.

Thank you so much for always encouraging me to do my best and be who God created me to be. I appreciate you all so very incredibly much!

Chapter 1

Introduction

Chapter 1: Introduction

Welcome to your guide on maximizing tax deductions for self-employed and gig economy workers. Whether you drive for Uber, deliver food with Door Dash, host on Airbnb, create content on YouTube, or sell on Etsy, understanding how to track and claim your expenses is essential for minimizing your tax liability.

This guide aims to help you obtain the maximum refund possible or, at the very least, pay the least amount in taxes. This is not a guide the IRS would want me to share with you because it reveals exactly what you can and cannot deduct as a small business owner in the gig economy.

Drawing from my 17 years of experience in saving my clients money, I am here to help you start saving money yourself. During my career as a tax professional, I have served a diverse range of clients, preparing all kinds of taxes, from regular W2 1040s to Schedule C's and K1s. I have worked for multiple corporations preparing taxes, managed tax offices, and served as the go-to expert for other tax preparers, especially when it came to Small Business Schedule C's, K1s, truckers' taxes, minister taxes, stocks, and day traders' taxes.

I am bringing together all my experience to help you save money and get the most out of your business expenses and tax deductions. If there is a tax deduction or a way to save you money, I WILL find it!

This book is here to help you navigate the often-confusing world of tax deductions and ensure you keep as much of your hard-earned money as possible.

Chapter 2

Understanding Business Expenses

Chapter 2: Understanding Business Expenses

Section 162 of the Internal Revenue Code

Understanding self-employment or gig economy business expenses begins with Section 162 of the Internal Revenue Code (IRC). This section outlines the guidelines for business expenses, stating that businesses can deduct any expense that is both ordinary and necessary.

Section 162 specifically allows a business to deduct all ordinary and necessary expenses paid or incurred during the taxable year while carrying on any trade or business.

Key Points of Section 162:

- Ordinary Expenses: These are expenses common and accepted in your industry. They are customary and usual for the business or trade in which you are engaged.
- Necessary Expenses: These expenses are appropriate and helpful for your business. While they do not have to be indispensable, they must be appropriate and useful for the business.

Examples of Deductible Expenses Under Section 162:

- Rent: Payments for the use of property for your business.
- Salaries and Wages: Payments to employees for their services.
- Supplies: Costs of supplies consumed during business.
- Repairs and Maintenance: Costs of keeping your property in good operating condition.
- Advertising: Expenses for promoting your business.
- Travel: Costs of business travel away from your home.

Purpose of Section 162:

The primary purpose of Section 162 is to allow businesses to deduct necessary and ordinary expenses, thereby reducing their taxable income.

This helps ensure that businesses are taxed only on their net income after accounting for the costs of generating that income.

Understanding Section 162 is crucial for business owners, including those in the gig economy, as it helps them identify which expenses can be legitimately deducted, reducing their tax liability.

Criteria for Deductible Business Expenses:

To be deductible, a business expense must meet these criteria:

- Ordinary: An expense is considered ordinary if it is common and accepted in your industry. Most business owners in the same field would typically incur these expenses.

- Necessary: An expense is considered necessary if it is helpful and appropriate for your trade or business. It does not have to be indispensable to qualify as necessary.

Clearer Definitions:

- Ordinary: The expense is typical and widely accepted within your industry.
- Necessary: The expense is appropriate and helpful, contributing to the effective management of your business.

If an expense meets both the ordinary and necessary criteria, it can be deducted as a business expense, making it tax-deductible.

Business expenses are the operating costs of running a business. Identifying which costs qualify as business expenses is crucial because these expenses are tax-deductible, whereas other types of expenses are not.

Tracking Your Business Expenses

Now that we understand that expenses must be ordinary and necessary for the business to be tax-deductible, let us discuss how to keep track of your expenses.

Tracking your expenses is straightforward. Start by getting a notebook. Each day, write the date at the top of a page and list everything you purchased for your business on that date. This requires some discipline, but it is essential because it counts as written proof in the eyes of the IRS.

Make sure to include the date on each page and document every single purchase related to your business. This includes anything bought to operate, manage, or market your business—if it is ordinary and necessary, write it down.

Managing Uncertain Expenses

When you are unsure if an item is tax-deductible for your business, it is best to err on the side of caution and write it down anyway. Keep a detailed record of the expenses, and when it is time to prepare your taxes, bring your records to me. I will review these uncertain items and provide guidance on whether they can be deducted. My goal is to help you navigate the complexities of tax deductions, ensuring you maximize your savings while staying compliant with tax regulations.

My goal is always to make sure that you get the best refund possible! If that is not possible then my next option is to zero you out so that you do not have to pay any taxes, and if that absolutely cannot happen then my last thing is to make it where you pay the absolute most definitely least possible taxes.

Utilizing Expense Tracking Tools

If manual tracking is not your preference, there are various tools and services available to streamline the process. Here are a few options:

- **QuickBooks**: A popular accounting software that offers comprehensive expense tracking, invoicing, and financial management features tailored for small businesses.
- **Wave**: A free, user-friendly accounting tool that provides expense tracking, invoicing, and receipt scanning capabilities.
- **FreshBooks**: An accounting solution designed for freelancers and small business owners, featuring time tracking, invoicing, and expense management.
- **Accounting Firms**: Professional accounting firms can manage your expense tracking and bookkeeping, ensuring accuracy and compliance.

Personalized Assistance

If you need personalized assistance with your expense tracking, feel free to contact me. I can help you set up a system that works best for your business, whether it involves using software, maintaining manual records, or a combination of both. My experience and expertise in tax preparation and economic management will provide you with the support you need to keep your finances organized and optimized for tax deductions.

Benefits of Accurate Expense Tracking

Accurate expense tracking offers numerous benefits beyond tax deductions:

- **Improved Cash Flow**: By keeping track of expenses, you can better manage your cash flow, ensuring you have enough funds to cover your operating costs.
- **Tax Savings**: Diligent expense tracking helps identify all deductions, reducing your taxable income and increasing your tax savings.
- **Spending Trends**: Regularly monitoring expenses allows you to identify spending trends, helping you make informed financial decisions.
- **Error and Fraud Detection**: Keeping detailed records helps detect discrepancies or fraudulent activities early, protecting your business from potential losses.
- **Financial Planning**: Accurate records support effective financial planning, helping you set realistic budgets and achieve your business goals.

By leveraging these tools and resources, you can ensure that your business expenses are meticulously tracked and accurately reported, maximizing your tax deductions, and enhancing your overall financial health.

Tips for Effective Expense Tracking:

- **Business Expense Tracking**: Accurate tracking is key to maintaining financial records and maximizing tax deductions.
- **Business Bank Account**: Separating personal and business finances simplifies tracking and reporting.
- **Accounting Software**: Automate your expense tracking to save time and reduce errors.
- **Record Keeping**: The IRS generally requires you to keep expense receipts for three years.
- **Benefits**: Tracking expenses improves cash flow, helps with tax savings, identifies spending trends, detects potential errors or fraud, and supports financial planning.

Practical Example:

Some of my clients take pictures of their receipts and email them to a dedicated business expense email account. At the end of the year, they have all their receipts in one place, making it easy to calculate expenses and provide them for tax filing.

By keeping meticulous records, you ensure that you can substantiate your deductions and make the most of your business expenses for tax purposes.

Chapter 3

Fully Deductible Expenses

Chapter 3: Fully Deductible and Partially Deductible Expenses

Understanding which business expenses are fully deductible and which are only partially deductible is crucial for maximizing your tax savings. In this chapter, we will explore these categories, starting with expenses that are always fully deductible.

Fully Deductible Expenses

Certain business expenses can be deducted in full, reducing your taxable income. Here are some of the most common fully deductible expenses:

- **Advertising and Marketing**: All expenses related to advertising and marketing, such as online ads, promotional materials, and marketing campaigns, are fully deductible.
- **Processing Fees**: Fees charged by business accounts for processing transactions or using corporate credit cards are fully deductible.
- **Education and Training**: Costs for education and training for yourself or your employees, including courses, workshops, and seminars, are fully deductible.
- **Legal Fees**: Some legal fees, such as those for business-related legal advice and services, are fully deductible.
- **Licenses and Regulatory Fees**: Fees for business licenses and regulatory compliance are fully deductible.
- **Wages**: Payments made to contract employees or freelancers are fully deductible.

- **Employee Benefit Programs**: Costs associated with employee benefit programs, including health insurance and retirement plans, are fully deductible.
- **Equipment Rentals**: Renting equipment necessary for your business operations is fully deductible.
- **Business Insurance**: Premiums paid for business insurance policies are fully deductible.
- **Office Expenses and Supplies**: Expenses for office supplies and general office operations are fully deductible.
- **Maintenance and Repair Costs**: Costs for maintaining and repairing business property and equipment are fully deductible.
- **Office Lease**: Leasing office space for your business is fully deductible.
- **Utility Expenses**: Utilities such as electricity, water, and internet services for your business office are fully deductible.
- **Business Bank Account Fees**: Fees and interest on business bank accounts are fully deductible, provided the account is used solely for business purposes.
- **Digital Downloads**: Purchases of digital products such as fonts, software, and other digital tools for business use are fully deductible.

Partially Deductible Expenses

Some expenses that are both personal and business-related can only be partially deducted. This means you can only deduct the portion of the expense that is directly related to your business. Here are some examples and guidelines:

- **Mixed-Use Expenses**: If an expense serves both personal and business purposes, only the business-related portion is deductible. For instance, if you use your personal car for both personal and business trips, you can only deduct the mileage or expenses related to business use.
- **Travel Expenses**: Business travel expenses are deductible, but if your trip includes personal activities, only the business-related costs are deductible. For example, if you travel to Los Angeles for a business conference but spend a day at Disneyland, the cost of your flight to LA and the hotel during the conference are deductible, but your Disneyland tickets are not.
- **Home Office**: If you use part of your home for business, you can deduct a portion of your home expenses, such as rent, utilities, and insurance, based on the percentage of your home used for business.

A little tip that not many people know, however I like to tell my clients because I like my clients to save money. If you had a small window vinyl or a magnet on your vehicle then every single mile you drive that vehicle is counted as business miles. How could that be, you ask? Because it is advertising! So, all you must do is get a small window vinyl or a small magnet or even a big magnet if you want to and always keep it on your vehicle then every single mile driven on that vehicle is a deduction.

Important Considerations

- **Documentation**: Maintain detailed records and receipts for all expenses. Proper documentation is crucial to substantiate your deductions in case of an IRS audit.

- **Business Purpose**: Ensure that expenses are primarily for business purposes to qualify for deductions. Personal expenses are not deductible.
- **Consultation**: When in doubt about whether an expense is deductible, consult with a tax professional. They can provide guidance and help you navigate complex tax regulations.

By understanding and accurately categorizing your business expenses, you can maximize your deductions and minimize your tax liability. This chapter has covered fully deductible expenses and provided insights into handling partially deductible expenses, helping you make informed financial decisions for your business.

Chapter 4

Non-deductible Expenses

Chapter 4: Non-Deductible Expenses

Personal vs. Business Expenses

It is essential to distinguish between personal and business expenses. Any expense that benefits you personally rather than your business is non-deductible.

For example, if you travel to Los Angeles for business and spend a day at Disneyland, the park tickets are not deductible. However, your flight to LA can be deductible if you can prove that most of your time was spent on business activities.

Gray Areas in Deductions

Navigating the gray areas of deductions can be tricky. The key is to ensure that the primary purpose of the expense is business-related. Always keep detailed records and be prepared to justify the business necessity of the expense if questioned by the IRS.

Non-Deductible Expenses for Small Businesses

Generally, the following expenses are not tax-deductible:

- **Some Taxes**: Certain taxes that are not directly related to your business operations.
- **Fines and Penalties**: Any fines or penalties imposed for legal violations.
- **Some Insurance**: Premiums for personal insurance policies, such as life insurance.
- **Commuting Costs**: Expenses related to commuting from home to your regular place of business.
- **Home Office Fees**: General household expenses that do not qualify under the home office deduction rules.
- **Personal and Family Expenses**: Costs that are personal in nature and do not have a business purpose.
- **Charitable Contributions**: Contributions made to charities are not deductible as business expenses, but they may be deductible as personal charitable contributions.
- **Political Contributions**: Donations made to political campaigns or candidates.
- **Anything Illegal**: Expenses incurred for illegal activities or items.
- **Gifts Over $25**: The portion of any gift given to a single person over $25.
- **Some Meals**: Meals that are considered lavish or extravagant, or that do not meet the IRS guidelines for business meal deductions.
- **Business Travel Expenses for Additional Travelers**: Travel costs for family members or others who are not directly involved in the business purpose of the trip.

By understanding what expenses are non-deductible, you can better manage your finances and ensure compliance with tax regulations. Always consult with a tax professional if you have questions about specific expenses and their deductibility.

Chapter 5
The Gig Economy Explained

Chapter 5: The Gig Economy Explained

What is a Gig Economy Job?

In understanding the gig economy, it is important to define what constitutes a gig economy job. The gig economy refers to a labor market where individuals engage in short-term, project-based work rather than traditional full-time employment.

A gig economy job encompasses a wide range of roles found on platforms like Uber, Door Dash, Lyft, Instacart, and various gig websites such as Craigslist. It also includes freelance work like blogging, vlogging, and other online gig platforms. Essentially, any job that involves temporary or freelance work, facilitated through digital platforms, falls under the gig economy umbrella.

In this ever-changing economy, gig work has become increasingly popular. Many people will have a regular full-time job and then do gig work on the side. For instance, I have many clients that work full time Monday through Friday 9:00 to 5:00 job and then on the weekends will either do door dash or Uber. As prices rise in our economy today it has become necessary for people to take on two and three, sometimes four distinct types of gig economy jobs just to make ends meet nowadays.

This started becoming immensely popular and ever prevalent during the pandemic and has continued even now.

Characteristics of the Gig Economy

The gig economy is characterized by:

- **Flexibility**: Workers have the freedom to choose when and where they work, often setting their own schedules.
- **Temporary and Part-Time Positions**: Jobs are typically short-term or project-based, with no long-term commitment.
- **Independent Contractors and Freelancers**: Individuals are often independent contractors or freelancers, responsible for their own taxes and benefits.
- **Digital Platforms**: Work is frequently obtained through online platforms that connect workers with clients or customers seeking services.

Benefits and Drawbacks

Benefits:

- **Flexibility**: Workers can adapt their schedules to personal needs or fluctuating demand.
- **Accessibility**: Easy entry into the job market with minimal startup costs.
- **Diverse Opportunities**: Wide range of roles and industries available for gig workers.

Now that we have established some benefits of gig economy jobs we will also talk about drawbacks of these types of jobs.

Drawbacks:

- **Lack of Job Security**: Gig workers often face uncertainty in terms of income stability and job continuity.

- **No Paid Benefits**: Typically, gig workers do not receive benefits such as health insurance, paid vacation, or sick leave.
- **Income Variability**: Earnings can fluctuate based on demand and hours worked.
- **Isolation**: Working independently can lead to feelings of isolation or loneliness.

Key Takeaways

- The gig economy offers flexibility and accessibility to both workers and businesses, catering to the demands of a modern, flexible lifestyle.
- It encompasses a diverse range of jobs beyond traditional perceptions, including services like ridesharing, food delivery, freelancing, and short-term lodging.
- The gig economy is expanding rapidly, reflecting changing workforce dynamics and technological advancements.
- There are many advantages taxwise in this field.

Common Gig Economy Platforms

Some of the most prominent gig economy platforms include:

- **Ridesharing**: Uber, Lyft
- **Food Delivery**: Door Dash, Uber Eats, Instacart
- **Lodging**: Airbnb
- **Freelancing**: Upwork, Fiverr
- **E-commerce**: Etsy, eBay, Shopify

Understanding the gig economy is essential for navigating the evolving landscape of work opportunities and ensuring informed decisions about employment and entrepreneurship in the digital age.

Chapter 6

Tracking Your Expenses

Chapter 6: Tracking Your Expenses

The Importance of Record-Keeping

Now that we have identified what qualifies as a business expense and explored the nature of gig economy jobs, let's delve into the critical task of tracking your expenses. Effective record-keeping is essential for maintaining financial clarity and ensuring compliance with tax regulations.

To start, all you need is a simple notebook. Begin each page by writing the date at the top and meticulously list every purchase made that day. This disciplined approach serves as crucial written proof in the event of an IRS audit. Remember to document every expense related to the operation, marketing, or management of your business.

Tools for Tracking Expenses

For those who prefer digital solutions, numerous apps and software are available to streamline expense tracking:

- **QuickBooks**: A comprehensive accounting software package tailored for small businesses, offering robust features for expense management and financial reporting.
- **Expensify**: An intuitive app designed to simplify expense tracking and management, with features for capturing receipts, categorizing expenses, and generating expense reports.
- **Wave**: free accounting software that includes powerful expense tracking capabilities, ideal for small business owners looking to manage finances effectively.

Choosing the Right Tool

Selecting the right expense tracking tool depends on your specific business needs and preferences. Consider factors such as ease of use, integration with other financial systems, and the level of support provided. Digital tools not only streamline the tracking process but also enhance accuracy and organization, facilitating better economic management overall.

Benefits of Digital Expense Tracking

- **Efficiency**: Automates data entry and simplifies expense categorization.
- **Accuracy**: Reduces human error associated with manual record-keeping.
- **Accessibility**: Access expense records anytime, anywhere, using mobile devices or desktop computers.
- **Compliance**: Ensures adherence to tax regulations by maintaining detailed and organized records.
- **Financial Insights**: Provides valuable insights into spending patterns, enabling informed budgeting and expense control.

Whether opting for traditional pen-and-paper methods or embracing digital solutions, diligent expense tracking is a cornerstone of financial responsibility for gig economy workers and small business owners alike. By maintaining accurate records, you not only optimize tax deductions but also gain valuable insights into your business's financial health and growth opportunities. Choose the method that best suits your business operations and commit to consistent and thorough record-keeping practices.

Chapter 7

Rideshare Drivers

Chapter 7: Specific Deductions for Rideshare Drivers

Unique Expenses for Rideshare Drivers

Rideshare driving, such as with Uber and Lyft, is a prominent gig economy job with its own set of unique expenses eligible for tax deductions. Understanding these deductions can significantly impact your tax liability, potentially resulting in a larger refund or lower taxes owed.

Rideshare drivers are classified as self-employed, allowing them to claim various tax deductions related to their business activities. This includes expenses specific to driving passengers, whether through rideshare platforms or as independent contractor cab or limo drivers.

Common Deductible Expenses

- **Advertising Expenses**: Costs incurred for advertising your services are fully deductible.
- **Platform Fees**: Fees charged by rideshare platforms like Uber and Lyft are deductible business expenses. These fees are typically detailed in reports provided by the platforms, making them easy to track for tax purposes.
- **Mileage**: Keeping track of miles driven while online and available for ride requests is crucial. This includes miles driven to areas with higher client demand, such as driving from Lakeland, FL, to Orlando, FL. All these miles are deductible, but meticulous record-keeping is essential to substantiate claims.
- **Car Maintenance**: Expenses such as car washes, detailing, and regular maintenance to keep your vehicle in top condition for passengers are deductible.

- **Client Amenities**: Providing amenities like cold bottled water, ice packs, or even vomit bags enhance customer experience and qualifies as a deductible expense.
- **Coolers**: If you purchase coolers to keep the water cold as well as the ice packs to keep the water cold those are also a deductible expense.
- **Cleaning Products and Air Fresheners**: Items used to maintain a clean and pleasant vehicle environment for passengers are deductible.
- **Snacks**: Offering snacks or gum or mints to passengers can improve ratings and is considered a deductible expense.
- **Phone and Accessories**: Necessary items like mobile phones, chargers, mounts, and apps used exclusively for business purposes are deductible. Additionally, a portion of your cell phone bill may be deductible based on business use. Keep in mind that it is only your part of the cell phone bill not the other family members or people on that same cell phone bill.
- **Tolls and Parking Fees**: Expenses for tolls and parking incurred during business activities are deductible.
- **First Aid or Roadside Assistance Kits**: Essential safety kits are not only prudent but also deductible as business expenses.

Considerations for Vehicle Expenses

- **Claiming Miles**: Instead of itemizing gas receipts and other vehicle expenses, claiming mileage driven for business purposes simplifies deductions and is often more advantageous.

- **Vehicle Costs**: While car insurance and loan payments for personal use are not deductible, expenses directly related to business use can be claimed.

Rideshare drivers have access to a range of tax deductions that can significantly reduce taxable income. By carefully documenting and categorizing expenses throughout the year, drivers can maximize deductions while ensuring compliance with IRS guidelines. These deductions not only help offset the costs of operating a rideshare business but also contribute to overall financial efficiency and profitability.

Understanding and leveraging these deductions is essential for rideshare drivers seeking to optimize their tax situation and maximize their earnings from gig economy work. Regularly consulting with a tax professional can further ensure that you are taking full advantage of all available deductions and complying with tax regulations.

Chapter 8

Food Delivery Drivers

Chapter 8: Specific Deductions for Food Delivery Drivers

Unique Expenses for Food Delivery Drivers

Food delivery services like Instacart, Door Dash, Uber Eats, Grubhub, and Postmates have become integral parts of the gig economy. If you participate in delivering food through these platforms, it is crucial to understand the specific tax deductions available to you. This knowledge can help you optimize your tax strategy and potentially reduce your tax liability.

Common Deductible Expenses

- **Mileage**: Keeping meticulous records of the miles driven for business purposes is essential. This includes tracking trips from your home to busier areas where you are likely to receive more delivery requests. Each mile driven for work is tax-deductible and should be recorded daily.
- **Coolers and Insulated Bags**: These items are necessary to maintain the temperature of food during delivery and qualify as deductible expenses.
- **Platform Fees**: Like rideshare drivers, fees charged by food delivery platforms are deductible business expenses.
- **Car Maintenance**: Costs associated with car washes, detailing, and upkeep to ensure a clean and odor-free vehicle are deductible.
- **Phone and Accessories**: Since your phone is indispensable for receiving orders and navigating deliveries, expenses related to your phone, such as chargers, mounts, and Bluetooth devices, are deductible. A portion of your phone bill attributable to business use is also deductible.

- **Apps**: Any applications purchased specifically for managing your food delivery business are eligible for tax deductions.
- **Cleaning Supplies**: Items like trash bags and cleaning products used to maintain your vehicle's cleanliness are deductible.
- **Personal Protective Equipment (PPE)**: Necessary safety gear, such as masks and gloves, required for your job is tax-deductible.
- **First Aid Kit and Roadside Assistance**: These kits are essential for emergencies and qualify as deductible business expenses.
- **Inspections and Background Checks**: Any costs incurred for vehicle inspections or background checks mandated by the delivery platform are deductible.

Chapter 9

Airbnb Hosts

Chapter 9: Specific Deductions for Airbnb Hosts

Unique Expenses for Airbnb Hosts

The Airbnb gig economy offers unique opportunities and expenses that hosts can deduct to optimize their tax situation. Whether you are already hosting or considering becoming an Airbnb host, understanding these deductions can significantly impact your financial planning and tax liabilities.

Common Deductible Expenses

- **Startup Fees**: Any initial fees paid to join Airbnb or set up your hosting business, including website fees, are tax-deductible.
- **Special Modifications**: Costs incurred to make your property more accessible or suitable for guests, such as wheelchair ramps or widened doorways, are deductible.
- **Remodels**: Expenses related to structural changes or expansions made to accommodate guests, like opening spaces or adding rooms, qualify as deductions.
- **Furniture and Bedding**: Beds, mattresses, and other furniture purchased specifically for guests are deductible, as are decorative items to enhance guest experience.
- **Games and Equipment**: Expenses for entertainment items or equipment provided for guest use, such as board games or exercise equipment, are deductible.
- **Pool Installation and Maintenance**: Costs associated with installing a pool to attract guests, along with ongoing maintenance expenses, are deductible.

- **Internet and Cable**: A percentage of expenses for providing internet and cable services to guests, as well as related home utilities, are deductible.
- **Food and Prepared Meals**: Costs for providing food or prepared meals for guests are deductible.
- **Insurance**: Additional insurance coverage purchased for hosting activities, along with property taxes and a portion of mortgage payments, are deductible.
- **Household Goods**: Everyday items like toilet paper and other supplies provided for guest use are deductible.
- **Extra Keys or Key Boxes**: Expenses for additional keys or secure key boxes purchased for guest convenience are deductible.
- **Cleaning Supplies and Services**: Costs for cleaning supplies or hiring cleaning services between guest stays are deductible.
- **Guest Amenities**: Expenses for providing toiletries, snacks, bottled water, welcome gifts, and pool supplies for guest enjoyment are deductible.
- **Air Fresheners and Cleaning Products**: Products used to maintain a pleasant environment for guests, such as air fresheners or cleaning supplies, are deductible.
- **Laundry Supplies**: Expenses for laundry detergents and fabric softeners used for guest laundry facilities are deductible.
- **Utilities**: A percentage of utilities like electricity and water used by guests are deductible based on the portion used for hosting activities.
- **Extras for Better Reviews**: Additional amenities purchased to enhance guest satisfaction and improve reviews, such as welcome baskets or streaming services, are deductible.
- **Printer and Copier Supplies**: Paper and ink used by guests for printing or copying are deductible if provided by the host.

Calculating Percentages

If determining the percentage of expenses used for business purposes is challenging, consider this example: Suppose most of your home is available for guest use except for a private area like a bedroom. In this case, you may be able to claim 80% to 90% of your property expenses as deductible.

Example: I have a client who is very invested in Airbnb. She gives her guests the full range of the entire house except for her bedroom alone. So that is 90% of the house that is used for guests, so that is the communal area for her to claim all the expenses in.

Understanding and meticulously documenting these deductible expenses can ensure you maximize your tax deductions as an Airbnb host. Keeping detailed records throughout the year will help substantiate your deductions in case of an IRS audit, providing peace of mind and financial benefits for your hosting business.

Chapter 10

Freelancers & Influencers

Chapter 10: Specific Deductions for Video Freelancers and Influencers

Unique Expenses for Video Freelancers

Video freelancers and influencers encompass a diverse range of professionals, including vloggers, YouTubers, personal coaches, singers, entertainers, financial advisors, and anyone who frequently appears on camera. Their work is often centered around their public image and presentation, which makes certain expenses uniquely deductible for them. This chapter delves into specific tax deductions available to this group, focusing on how their business activities, which revolve around maintaining a polished and professional appearance, can impact their tax filings.

Common Deductible Expenses

- **Hair and Makeup Products**: Maintaining a professional appearance is crucial for video freelancers. Expenses for haircuts, hairstyles, hair treatments, and makeup products are deductible. This includes regular grooming services, hair dye, extensions, and any other products used to achieve a specific look required for their business.
- **Facial Hair Grooming**: For male influencers or public speakers with facial hair, grooming products such as beard oils, trimmers, and other maintenance items are deductible as they contribute to their professional appearance.
- **Makeup and Nails**: For female freelancers, makeup and nail care are deductible. This includes the cost of cosmetics, manicures, artificial nails, acrylics, and any

other products used to maintain a polished look essential for their on-camera presence.

- **Skincare Products**: Keeping their skin in optimal condition is important for video professionals. Expenses for skincare products like cleansers, moisturizers, and treatments are deductible as they contribute to maintaining a professional appearance.
- **Foot Care and Pedicures**: Public speakers and performers who spend considerable time on their feet can deduct the cost of foot care treatments and pedicures, recognizing the importance of comfort and appearance in their roles.
- **Video Equipment**: Essential equipment for video production, such as cameras, lighting, microphones, and tripods, can be depreciated over time. These expenses are deductible as they are related to creating video content.
- **Conferences and Educational Materials**: Attending industry conferences, workshops, and seminars, as well as purchasing educational materials such as books and online courses, are deductible. These expenses contribute to professional development and staying current in their field. Networking events also fall into this category as they provide opportunities for business growth and learning.

Real-Life Examples

To illustrate, let us consider a couple of real-life examples from my clients:

- Southern Gospel Singer: One client, a southern gospel singer, had specific stage costumes required for her performances. These costumes, which were not worn outside of her stage work, were fully deductible. Additionally, her makeup and hairstyling expenses were necessary to maintain a particular image, making them deductible as well.

- Keynote Speaker: Another client, a keynote speaker specializing in financial advancement, required a prominent level of professional appearance. Her expenses for hair weaves, business attire, and makeup were all tax-deductible because they contributed to her professional brand and stage presence.

So, if you are a video freelancer or influencer, do not hesitate to invest in that high-quality lipstick or professional wardrobe. As long as it is essential for maintaining your brand and appearance, it is a tax write-off!

Understanding and tracking these expenses accurately can help video freelancers and influencers optimize their tax returns. Detailed record-keeping and a clear understanding of what qualifies as a deduction are crucial for maximizing tax benefits and ensuring compliance with IRS regulations.

Chapter 11

Online Sellers

Chapter 11: Specific Deductions for Online Sellers

Unique Expenses for Online Sellers

In this chapter, we will focus on online sellers—those who use platforms like Facebook Marketplace, eBay, Etsy, Shopify, and related sites to sell products. Like other gig workers, online sellers have their own set of unique expenses that can be deducted from their taxes.

Common Deductible Expenses

- **Third-Party Payment Processing Fees**: Fees charged by payment processors (like PayPal or Stripe) are tax-deductible.
- **Platform Fees**: Fees charged by the selling platforms themselves, such as listing fees or transaction fees, are also deductible.
- **Phone and Service**: Cell phone expenses, including service charges, are deductible up to the percentage used for business purposes. This deduction applies only to your phone bill, not to family members' phone bills.
- **Mileage**: Deductible miles include those driven for business purposes, such as picking up items or supplies. Always keep a detailed log of your business-related miles.
- **Supplies for Packaging and Shipping**: Expenses for packaging materials and shipping costs are deductible. This includes boxes, tape, and any other materials used to prepare items for shipment.
- **Online Advertising**: Costs associated with online advertising, such as social media ads or Google ads, are tax-deductible.

- **Camera Equipment**: Any camera equipment purchased for taking product photos is deductible.
- **Conventions and Conferences**: Fees and travel expenses related to conventions and conferences for networking or purchasing from vendors are also deductible.

Example Scenario

Imagine you are an online seller who uses Facebook Marketplace and eBay to sell handmade crafts. Here is how some of these deductions might apply:

- You pay a fee to Facebook Marketplace for listing your products—this fee is deductible.
- You purchase a new camera to take high-quality photos of your crafts—this equipment is tax-deductible.
- You drive to a local craft store to buy packaging materials and pick up supplies—those miles are deductible.
- You attend a craft convention to network and source new materials. The registration fee and travel expenses for this event are also deductible.

Chapter 12

Conclusion

Chapter 12: Conclusion

Understanding and tracking business expenses is crucial for self-employed individuals and gig economy workers. By keeping detailed records and understanding what can be deducted, you can minimize your tax liability and maximize your deductions. My goal is to ensure you get the maximum refund legally possible or, if not, to zero out your tax liability. If neither is possible, my aim is to ensure you pay the least amount of taxes legally possible. If you need further assistance, stay tuned for the personal services I provide, which can be conducted entirely remotely.

—-

This book aims to empower you with the knowledge to effectively manage your business expenses and optimize your tax deductions. Thank you for taking the time to read, and I hope you find this information valuable in your self-employment journey.

If you would like further help, I provide different services that can be of value, especially when you own your own business. I provide tax services of course, this is also the first book in a series that will also be paperback, and I provide bookkeeping services as well on a retainer. If you would like to take advantage of my services, you can e-mail me with what your needs are, and I will provide you with the fees that will also be tax deductions to help meet those needs.

My e-mail is taxtipswithJenn at gmail.com.

About the Author

Jenn Davis has been a Tax Professional, saving her clients money for 17 years. Her motto is: "If there is a tax deduction or a way to save you money, I WILL find it!" She is a PTIN holder, and she is a part of the IRS registry for tax preparers. She has worked in different corporate settings for brand name companies and was the go-to for many of the preparers there to help with finding every deduction possible. She specializes in small business owners, Schedule C, self-employed entrepreneurs, gig economy workers, 1099'd independent contractors, truckers, and ministers; as well as any other 1040 taxes.

https://www.instagram.com/jennthetaxpro?igsh=MXc4dXZlN3J4YnBoag==

https://www.facebook.com/jennthetaxpro?mibextid=ZbWKwL

https://www.linkedin.com/in/jenn-davis-taxpro